My First Book of Wisconsin Snakes

by Jean Krieg

Hello!

Thank you for choosing this children's picture book. I think snakes are fascinating, yet under-appreciated reptiles. I hope this book sparks an interest in snakes!
Jean Krieg

Acknowledgements:

Thank you to Rori Paloski, Wisconsin Department of Natural Resources (WDNR) for her review.

Except where noted* the information in this book was obtained from WDNR link http://dnr.wi.gov/topic/WildlifeHabitat/herps.asp?mode=table&group=Snakes

* Snake length was obtained from:
  - http://eekwi.org/critter/reptile/index.htm for: Gophersnake, Gray (Black) Ratsnake, North American (Blue) Racer, Northern Ring-necked Snake, Plains Gartersnake, Prairie Ring-necked Snake, Timber Rattlesnake, Eastern Ribbonsnake
  - Wikipedia for: Lined Snake, Western Wormsnake

Status definitions:

  - Common: An abundant species found throughout a significant portion of the state
  - Special Concern: Problem of abundance or distribution is suspected but not yet proved
  - Endangered: Low and/or declining populations and are in need of conservation action

Image credits are listed at the end of the book.

Common Gartersnake

Status: Common   Length: 17-26 inches

Common Watersnake

Status: Common   Length: 24-40 inches

DeKay's Brownsnake

Status: Common   Length: 8-15 inches

Eastern Foxsnake

Status: Common   Length: 36-56 inches

Eastern Hog-nosed Snake

Status: Common   Length: 20-35 inches

Milksnake

Status: Common   Length: 24-36 inches

Red-bellied Snake

Status: Common   Length: 8-10 inches

Smooth Greensnake

Status: Common   Length: 14-20 inches

Butler's Gartersnake

Status: Special Concern   Length: 15-20 inches

Gophersnake

Status: Special Concern   Length: 50-80 inches

Gray (Black) Ratsnake

Status: Special Concern   Length: 40-72 inches

Lined Snake

Status: Special Concern   Length: 14-21 inches

North American (Blue) Racer

Status: Special Concern   Length: 36-72 inches

Northern Ring-necked Snake

Status: Special Concern   Length: 10-15 inches

Plains Gartersnake

Status: Special Concern   Length: 20-28 inches

Prairie Ring-necked Snake

Status: Special Concern   Length: 12-14 inches

Timber Rattlesnake

Status: Special Concern   Length: 36-56 inches

Western Wormsnake

Status: Special Concern   Length: 7.5-11 inches

Eastern Massasauga

Status: Endangered   Length: 20-32 inches

Eastern Ribbonsnake

Status: Endangered   Length: 18-26 inches

Queensnake

Status: Endangered   Length: 15-24 inches

Western Ribbonsnake

Status: Endangered   Length: 20-30 inches

About the Author:

Jean Krieg, a native of Wisconsin, is continually in awe of nature. She authored *My First Book of Common Wisconsin Birds* as her Wisconsin Master Naturalist Capstone project. Read her blog at https://mostlynaturestuff.wordpress.com/.

Wisconsin Master Naturalist: https://www.wimasternaturalist.org/

Resources to learn more about Wisconsin snakes:

1. Wisconsin Department of Natural Resources (WDNR): http://dnr.wi.gov/topic/WildlifeHabitat/herps.asp?mode=table&group=Snakes
2. Environment Education for Kids: http://eekwi.org/critter/reptile/index.htm

All images were obtained from Shutterstock.com except for the Butler's Gartersnake. Credits are as follows:

Common Gartersnake: Paul Reeves Photography
Common Watersnake: Psychotic Nature
DeKay's Brownsnake: Patrick K. Campbell
Eastern Foxsnake: Ryan M. Bolton
Eastern Hog-nosed Snake: Ryan M. Bolton
Milksnake: Jay Ondreicka
Red-bellied snake: Gerald A. DeBoer
Smooth greensnake: Fine Art Photos
Butler's Gartersnake: Rori Paloski, WDNR
Gophersnake: Anita Potter
Gray (Black) Ratsnake: steve52
Lined Snake: Psychotic Nature
North American (Blue) Racer: Psychotic Nature
Northern Ring-necked Snake: Meister Photos
Plains Gartersnake: Matt Jepson
Prairie Ring-necked Snake: Matt Jepson
Timber Rattlesnake: Matt Jepson
Western Wormsnake: Matt Jepson
Eastern Massasauga: Ryan M. Bolton
Eastern Ribbonsnake: Jay Ondreicka
Queensnake: Patrick K. Campbell
Western Ribbonsnake: Ryan M. Bolton

Front cover - Milksnake: Jay Ondreicka
Back cover – Common Gartersnake: Aneese